68
6

D1708886

BATS

BATS

ALICE L. HOPF

Illustrated with photographs by Dr. Merlin D. Tuttle

A Skylight Book

DODD, MEAD & COMPANY

New York

For MERLIN D. TUTTLE
who is fighting to save the bats of the world

ACKNOWLEDGMENT

The author wishes to acknowledge the help of Dr. Merlin D.
Tuttle for his work in reviewing the manuscript and for supplying
the many unique photographs that illustrate this book. Dr. Tuttle
is founder and president of Bat Conservation International, located
in the Milwaukee Public Museum, Milwaukee, Wisconsin 53233.

1 2 3 4 5 6 7 8 9 10

Library of Congress Cataloging in Publication Data

Hopf, Alice Lightner, date
   Bats.

   (A Skylight book)
   Includes index.
   Summary: Describes the characteristics, habits, and
natural environment of a variety of common and unusual
bats, the only mammals that fly.
   1. Bats—Juvenile literature.   [1. Bats]   I. Title.
QL737.C5H59 1985   599.4   84–28712
ISBN 0–396–08502–4

CONTENTS

A Chinese emperor's robe with a bat motif. The Metropolitan Museum of Art, Purchase, 1935, Joseph Pulitzer Bequest

1 BATS AND PEOPLE

How often have you seen a bat? Some people never see one in their whole lives. Most people think there are only a few kinds, but this is not so. Next to the rodents (mice, squirrels, beavers, and such), bats are the most numerous of all mammals. There are more than 950 kinds of bats (species, as the scientists say) in the world. They live on every continent, except Antarctica, and on many islands. And they come in a great variety of sizes and shapes with many different ways of life. But they are all bats and are the only mammal that can fly.

Many people are afraid of bats. This foolish fear goes back thousands of years, when people had superstitions about them. Some people still do. People are active in the daytime, but bats come out at night. Our ancestors were afraid of the dark, which they believed harbored witches and demons. So it was natural for them to think that bats were the servants of such evil spirits. This is why Halloween decorations feature bats flying along with the witches.

Bats seem unnatural and unstable to humans. As far back as the ancient Greeks, the storyteller Aesop told a tale about a bat that was captured by a weasel. The bat cried out that he was not a mouse, as the weasel thought, but a bird. So the weasel let him go. But some time later, when the weasel was hunting birds and caught the bat, that creature cried, "Can't you see I'm not a bird? I have no feathers." So the weasel let him go again.

The American Indians also have a story about the bat, in which the birds and the animals played a game of ball. The bat tried to play on both teams, for while he had fur and four legs like the mammals, he could fly like the birds. These myths show that people had an uncertain feeling about bats and that they distrusted and feared them.

On the other side of the world, however, people take the opposite view of bats. The Chinese word for bat is *fu*. And in Chinese writing, the sign that means *fu* also means *wu*, which is the Chinese word for happiness. Thus bats have always been associated with happiness and good luck. Bats are often used in Chinese paintings and designs, and there is a standard design of five bats, arranged in a circle, with wings outspread. It is known as the *wu-fu* and the design is often used in good-luck charms. Sometimes there is a little tree of life in the center, and Chinese people give such charms as gifts and wear them to ward off bad luck.

Bats living in the United States are quite small. They are mostly insect-eaters and are extremely useful. It has been estimated that one bat can catch five hundred or more mosquitoes in an hour. This is about one every seven seconds. On a dark night, a streetlight will often attract moths and other insects, and sometimes you can see a dark shape darting in and out among them. This may be a bat —one of the most useful animals in controlling insect pests.

The bat's wings are a development of its arms and

fingers. The forearm, from the elbow down, and the four fingers have been greatly lengthened, and a skinlike membrane, much like that on a duck's webbed foot, covers these bones. The thumb is kept free with a claw at the end for hanging, crawling, and manipulating. The web extends across all the fingers and back to the much shorter hind legs and feet. In some bats, the tail is also covered by the membrane, and in some it is not. In fact, some bats have no tails. But in all cases, the claws on the hind feet are free. This is necessary for bats, as they hang head downward from the branch of a tree or the roof of a cave.

2 ONE HUNDRED MILLION YEARS

The bat's lineage goes back millions of years. The earliest fossil of a bat so far discovered is some 50 million years old, yet it is much like the bats of today. How the bats developed wings is lost in the mists of time. Why do bats fly only at night? One theory is that when the mammals were displacing the dinosaurs, almost 100 million years ago, many insects took to flying at night to escape bird and reptile predators. At that time, the birds were just developing and there were still flying reptiles. These were all daytime creatures, so some insects found safety by flying at night. Then, as bats began to fly, they hunted at

A big brown bat (Eptesicus fuscus) *perched on a barn wall. This is one of the species most often encountered by people.* © Merlin D. Tuttle, Bat Conservation International, Milwaukee Public Museum

night when there was plenty of food to be found and they were safe from daytime predators.

The early bats were probably insect-eaters, as are most of our bats in the United States. But bats have learned to eat a variety of foods. In tropical areas many enjoy fruits and nectar from flowers, and some even catch fish or frogs. A very few drink blood or dine on smaller bats.

Most bats have well-furred bodies and without the wings look like little mice or, with the larger ones, like dogs or foxes. The German word for bat means "flying mouse." The Australians call their giant bats "flying foxes."

Many bats have strange flaps of skin on their faces, especially above the nose. These are called leaf-nosed bats. Most have a spearlike growth, called the tragus, standing upright inside each ear. These unusual decorations are believed to be connected with the bat's echolocation system, which will be discussed in another chapter.

Bats are mammals, as are all warm-blooded, furry animals that give birth to live offspring and feed them with the mother's milk. So are cats and dogs, cows and horses, lions and tigers, men and monkeys. But bats are more like men and monkeys than dogs and cats. This fact was noted by the great Swedish scientist Linnaeus when, in 1758, he was arranging his list of living creatures, a system that scientists still use today.

Most mammals suckle their young from nipples placed on the abdomen, near the hind legs. This is where a cow is milked. Only humans and monkeys and elephants—and bats—have the nipples on the chest. For this reason, Linnaeus at first placed the bats in a group very close to humans. But he soon recognized his mistake and shifted them to a special listing by themselves.

Scientists divide bats into two main groups: the Megachiroptera, or fruit-eating bats, and the Microchiroptera, or insect-eating bats. "Mega" means large and "micro" means small, while "chiroptera" is the scientific word for bat. It comes from two Greek words meaning "hand" and "wing." While the biggest bats are fruit bats and the insect-eaters are all quite small, still there are some little bats among the Megachiroptera and some fairly large ones among the Microchiroptera. Moreover, a number of the microbats are fruit-eaters, but none of the megabats eat insects.

All the megabats live in the Old World (Asia, Africa,

14

A D'Orbigny's round-eared bat (Tonatia sylvicola) *carrying a long-horned grasshopper. This species listens for the mating calls of its prey and may be able to identify them by their calls.* © Merlin D. Tuttle, Bat Conservation International, Milwaukee Public Museum

and Australia). There are none in the New World (North and South America). Thus, all our bats belong to the Microchiroptera group. Microbats are found all over the world and eat a great variety of food. Our ancestors, most of whom came here from various parts of Europe, knew only microbats, and those are the bats that you see in Halloween illustrations and that are mentioned in European literature. The great fruit bats, the flying foxes, live in Australia, India, and other parts of the East, countries that were unknown to our ancestors until explorers like Marco Polo and Magellan discovered them.

3 BATS AROUND THE WORLD

There are so many species of bats in our world (thirty-nine species in the United States alone), and they all have such long, scientific names, that I will describe only a few typical bats and use popular names whenever possible.

The small bats we know in the United States are similar to those found in Europe. Perhaps the most numerous are the little brown bats (*Myotis*). When their wings are stretched out, they are only about eight to twelve inches across. Their fur is mostly dull brown and the ears are erect and unfurred. The forearms and ears are usually black or brown.

Another kind of bat is the pipistrelle, of which there are

A hibernating eastern pipistrelle (Pipistrellus subflavus) *with its fur covered by condensed moisture droplets. This species hibernates individually in caves and is the one most often seen by cave explorers throughout eastern North America.* © Merlin D. Tuttle, Bat Conservation International, Milwaukee Public Museum

about a dozen species (two in North America and more in the Old World). In the United States, it is quite different. Its fur has a mottled, yellowish-brown tinge and the forearms and ears are yellowish. Another common bat is the big brown bat. Its wingspread is about twelve inches.

These three kinds of bats are all social animals. That is, they live in groups. They spend the day huddled in caves or some similar shelter, hanging upside down by their hind feet. When night comes, they fly out to catch insects.

We also have some solitary bats that like to live alone. They spend the day perched under leafy branches. They are known as tree bats, in contrast to cave bats, and in winter they migrate south like the birds. Among them is the red bat, a pretty animal, looking like a miniature red fox. Also we have the hoary bat that gets its name from the white hairs sprinkled over its reddish-brown fur. This is one of our most beautiful bats. Both these bats have short, round, well-furred ears.

Two unique bats live in the western United States: the spotted and the pallid bat. Both have very large ears and beautifully colored fur. The spotted bat is black with a

18

A pallid bat (Antrozous pallidus) *perched in a desert bush. All prey taken by this species is caught on the ground. Prey include a wide variety of crickets, katydids, scorpions, and even an occasional small lizard.* © Merlin D. Tuttle, Bat Conservation International, Milwaukee Public Museum

design of large white spots and has huge, pink ears. The pallid bat has a cream-colored body with large but slightly smaller ears.

As we go farther south in our country, we find different bats, including the fast-flying, free-tailed bats, which get their name from their unique, mouselike tails. The most unusual bats are found in the extreme Southwest, bordering on Mexico. These are related to the many tropical species. There we find the California mastiff bat, the leaf-chinned bat, and the California leaf-nosed bat. As their names show, they are strange-looking creatures compared with some of our plainer brown bats.

To see the most unusual-looking bats, one must go to the tropics. In Central and South America, we find the hare-lipped bats and the leaf-nosed bats, which have a great variety of leaflike protuberances growing from their noses. And here we also find the only true vampire bats.

When we move eastward around the world and come to Africa, we find more insect-eating bats, and also the many larger fruit-eating bats, the megabats. It is thought that bats moved from eating insects to eating fruit because they pursued insects into the flowers where they were feeding on nectar. In time, the bats took to eating nectar, too.

The biggest and most spectacular fruit bats are found in Asia, Australia, and neighboring islands like New Guinea. Even after almost three hundred years of exploration from Magellan and Columbus onward, Europeans did not know much about the creatures of the tropics. And as late as 1770, when the English explorer Captain James Cook visited Australia, that area was little known.

He had run his ship, *Endeavour*, onto a northern beach of Australia to make repairs. While work on the hull progressed and a botanist was drying plant specimens, a seaman was sent to look for water. Suddenly, the man came running back in a state of terror, crying that he had just seen the devil, as big as a gallon keg and with wings! When a scouting party was sent to look for the monster, they found a bat. What the Australians now call a flying fox, it is the largest of the bats and something unknown at that time in England.

There are flying foxes throughout most of the Old

World tropics, but the biggest and most astonishing ones are in the South Pacific. Their wingspans can be close to six feet and they have no tails. They do not have any of the weird facial decorations of the leaf-nosed bats, but have large, round eyes and do not use "sonar."

Portrait of an Indian flying fox (Pteropus giganteus). *Flying foxes play a critical role in seed dispersal and pollination of rain forest trees throughout much of the Old World.* © Merlin D. Tuttle, Bat Conservation International, Milwaukee Public Museum

4 EARS IN THE DARK

Perhaps the most remarkable thing about the bats was only discovered in this century. Some two hundred years ago, when modern science was just beginning, an Italian named Lazarro Spallanzani tried to learn how night-flying creatures find their way about without bumping into things. He soon discovered that owls cannot fly in absolute darkness, but that bats can. How are owls and bats different, he wondered? Even when he removed the eyes of some bats, they could still fly about and avoid slender threads hung from the roof of their cage. Moreover, when he took the blind bats some distance away and released them, they found their way back to their home roost. Even

24

A little brown bat (Myotis lucifugus) *in flight. This is one of the most common and widespread species of North American bats. Under ideal circumstances it can catch up to 900 insects in an hour, including many mosquitoes and other pest species. It hibernates in caves but often forms its nursery colonies in the attics and walls of buildings.* © Merlin D. Tuttle, Bat Conservation International, Milwaukee Public Museum

more remarkable, when he dissected the blind bats, he found their stomachs full of insects. Apparently, blind bats could hunt as well as sighted bats.

Spallanzani continued to experiment and tried plugging up the ears of his bats. In this condition, the bats released in the dark proved to be helpless. They could not navigate or catch insects. But how was it possible to substitute ears for eyes? Spallanzani never found out. The science of sound waves and electronics did not become well developed until the twentieth century.

In the late 1930s, a young scientist named Donald R. Griffin, working at Harvard and MIT, proved that bats make sounds. Not the little squeaking sounds that we sometimes hear, but ultrasonic sounds, too high for the human ear to perceive. Because of his work, we now know that **bats** send out these little clicks which bounce back to their **ears** from any object they strike, whether it be a wire **hanging** in front of the bat or a flying insect that is trying to escape. In this way, the bat sees with its ears and makes its way about the world of the dark.

Bats have used this system of echolocation for millions of years, but it was only discovered by humans in this century. About the same time that Griffin was solving the puzzle of the bat's ear, other scientists were developing sonar and radar systems that are used extensively today in ships and airplanes for military defense.

The bat's remarkable "sonar" is found mostly in the microbats, the insect-eating bats. No bats are blind, but megabats have exceptionally good eyesight and their food is waiting for them in the trees. They do not have to chase insects in the dark and so are far less dependent on sonar. Most use only their eyes.

Bats perform extraordinary aerial gymnastics while catching moths. Many moths can hear a bat approaching. In fact, scientists now know that they hear the bat's "sonar" clicks. An alerted moth promptly goes into a dive or a dodging flight, and may hide on the ground among the leaves. Some escape, but many are caught. Bats can use their wings like a net to catch an escaping moth.

5 WINTER STRATEGIES

All animals that do not live in the tropics must have some way of surviving the winter months. Mice and deer feed on grass, still green under the snow. But our bats eat insects and the flying insects disappear when winter comes. The bats have two choices: they can hibernate or they can migrate. Some species use one method and some the other.

Quite a few mammals go to sleep for the winter: bears and woodchucks and chipmunks. They either dig themselves a den or find some other animal's hole in the ground. But bats are not equipped with digging claws. The answer for them is a cave.

28

Caves are ideal places for bats to spend the winter. Cave temperatures are fairly constant and seldom go down to freezing. Bats usually choose a cave where the temperature ranges between 40° F and 48° F, although some prefer near-freezing temperatures. Bats hang head down from the ceiling and walls of the cave. As the cave temperature drops, the bat's body temperature also goes down, from about 104° to as low as 32°. The bats sleep and all their body functions slow down. Breathing goes from two hundred breaths a minute to as low as twenty-three. When bats start to hibernate, they are plump and fat from all the insects eaten during the summer. But by the time winter is over, they are very thin and must start feeding again.

Scientists who go into caves to study bats usually find several different species wintering in the same cave. Near the entrance there may be some big brown bats, hanging separately. These bats like to live alone. Farther in there may be a group of little brown bats, all clustered together. Looking like shriveled brown leaves, they cover large areas of walls and ceiling. Some caves may house hundreds of thousands of hibernating bats. The little pipistrelle bat is

Merlin Tuttle taking data on a gray bat (Myotis grisescens) *banded fourteen years earlier when it was a newly flying young. Bats, for their size, are extremely long-lived, some having been known to reach thirty years.*

also found wintering in caves but, being of a solitary nature, it does not gather in large groups.

Many species of bats are easily disturbed during hibernation. When people enter their caves in winter, bats wake up too often and exhaust their stored reserves of fat. Just a few disturbances can cause thousands of bats to starve before spring.

Since scientists began to band bats, a lot of interesting information has been gathered. The average life-span of a bat is twelve to fifteen years, but some bats have lived as long as thirty years. They come back to the same cave, often to the same spot in the cave. They sometimes find their way home from hundreds of miles away. Bats taken twenty-five miles out at sea and released have returned to their home roost.

Bats that do not hibernate must migrate to warmer regions for the winter. People were not aware of the extent of bat migrations until birdbanding became popular. When the great fall bird migrations got underway, scientists put up nets to catch the birds, which were then weighed, tagged, and released. While doing this work, birdbanders sometimes found bats in their nets, and they soon alerted bat scientists.

Batbanding was first done in caves, where there were thousands of hibernating bats. The batbanders needed only to go into the cave and pluck some off the walls. This type of work has now been abandoned because of the threat to the bats. Scientists who wanted to trace the bats' migrations had a more difficult time. They had to catch their bats as they flew south. Three of our American bat species migrate long distances: the red bat, the hoary bat, and the silver-haired bat. In our southwestern states, the Mexican free-tailed bat travels up to nine hundred miles south into Mexico to spend the winter. Many cave-dwelling bats also migrate, flying from their summer to their winter caves.

The problem with catching bats in nets, as is done with

A male red bat (Lasiurus borealis) *perched in a maple tree during its southward autumn migration along Lake Michigan. Red bats live solitary lives, roosting in tree foliage. They often hang by one foot, wrapped in their large furry tail membrane, mimicking a dead leaf. Like hoary bats, this species migrates north and south seasonally with the birds.* © Merlin D. Tuttle, Bat Conservation International, Milwaukee Public Museum

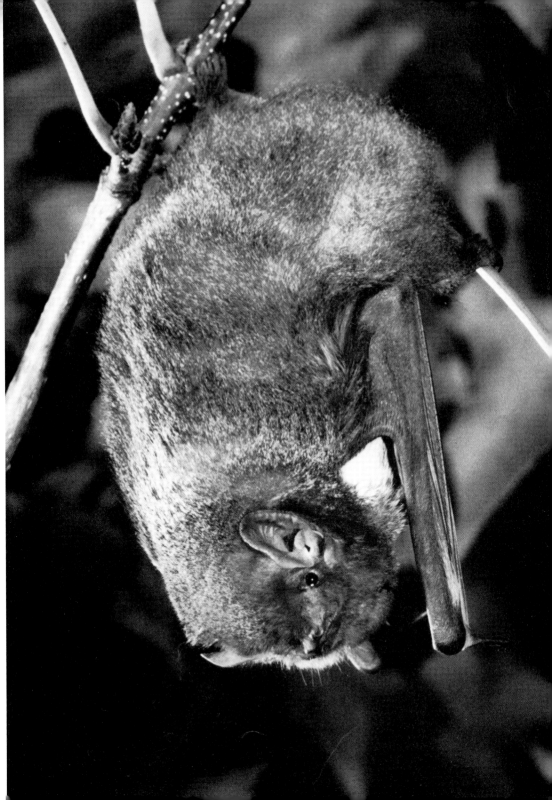

birds, is that the bat's "sonar" shows the bat where the net is in the darkness. While the birds fly into it, the bats avoid it. The Japanese have made some very fine "mist" nets that are good for trapping birds, which become entangled in the net without being hurt. Such nets have caught some bats, but not as many as desired.

We now know that bats often use the same flyways as the birds, sometimes flying right along with them in large numbers. These pathways usually follow some distinctive route, such as the Atlantic Coast or the Appalachian Mountain range.

In tropical countries, the insect-eating bats have little need to migrate. There is no winter weather and their food is more dependable. Fruit bats sometimes migrate from one area to another, according to when the fruit ripens. Fruit bats are much easier to catch, as most do not use "sonar" and fly into the nets.

6 MOTHERS AND BABIES

Some bats live in large groups, often thousands inhabiting one cave. But other species live alone or in small groups. Their courting and mating behavior is just as varied. In some cases, the male simply mates with as many females as he can and then leaves all care of the young to the mother. But in other species, the bats have elaborate courtship displays and may even mate for life. In recent years, scientists have observed some of the ways in which bats cooperate. For example, female vampire bats help each other rear their young and adopt orphans. Also vampires of either sex that fail to find food will be fed by others when they return to their roost.

With the megabats, which live in large groups, roosting in the same trees, it has been noticed that the nonbreeding adults usually stay on the fringes of the group, where they keep watch for any danger or disturbance. If they see a threat to the colony, they give loud alarm calls to alert the others. And when the bats fly off in search of food, they go in long lines with certain leaders in front.

Since hibernation begins soon after mating for our northern bats, the male's sperm does not immediately fertilize the egg, but stays in the mother's womb until spring. Or if an embryo is immediately formed, it does not begin to grow until the following spring. In some species, mating does not take place until spring, after the winter hibernation or migration. In the tropics, where there are fewer seasonal weather problems, some bats may have two breeding seasons.

The birth of a bat is a tricky business, but the mothers usually manage it successfully. By keeping captive pregnant bats, scientists have been able to watch the event. The usual resting posture of a bat is hanging upside-down by its hind feet. In many species of smaller bats, the mother moves around and takes hold also with her thumbs. She stretches herself out and curves her tail and wings under, thus forming a kind of cradle into which the baby bat falls. The baby begins to call as soon as its head appears. The mother licks the baby clean, holding on with a wing. Soon it makes its way to the nipple and begins to nurse. The whole process of birth takes about twenty minutes. Most baby bats are born naked, but in a short time they grow fur. Bats usually have only one baby a year, but a very few species, like our red bat, have two or more. Very young fruit-eating bats cling tightly to their mothers and are carried during searches for food. They cling to her breast with special hooked baby teeth. Insect-eating bats hang their babies in sheltered spots while hunting and return to care for them.

In our southwestern states, where the Mexican free-tailed bat (*Tadarida brasiliensis mexicana*) spends the summers, nursing mothers form huge colonies in caves of the region. In Bracken Cave in Texas, 20 million mother bats leave their babies (pups) hanging to the walls and ceiling while they forage for insects. Whenever a mother bat re-

A mother Mexican free-tailed bat (Tadarida brasiliensis) *with her newborn baby. Mother and baby will spend up to an hour getting to know each other's scent and vocalizations. Each mother usually produces just one young per year. Amazingly, she finds and nurses her own baby among the literally tons of others which roost on cave walls.* © Merlin D. Tuttle, Bat Conservation International, Milwaukee Public Museum

turns to nurse her baby, she must crawl over a multitude of others all struggling to be fed.

Scientists have assumed that the mothers could not find their own offspring among so many and so nursed the first baby they reached. But now Gary F. McCracken of the University of Tennessee has run blood tests on 167 mother bats and their pups. Only 17 percent were found to be nursing a strange pup. McCracken thinks that to find the right baby in such a huge gathering 83 percent of the time is pretty good. Watching through a "night scope," which magnifies the dim light several thousand times, scientists have seen how mother bats look for their babies. The mother lands where she left her pup and then calls and listens for an answer. Once she finds what she thinks is hers, she sniffs it all over to be sure.

Baby bats are fed milk until they can digest solid food. One expert suggests that mother bats may then feed them on partly digested insects, as some birds do. The babies have been seen to exercize their wings by beating them while roosting. Mothers may aid their youngsters in learning how to hunt, but this is still to be confirmed. Most appear to learn to fly on their own. In some places, if a baby loses its grip and falls from the mother or from its perch, it will die. Where possible, mothers rescue their babies.

There have been a number of interesting reports about devoted bat mothers rescuing their pups from people who had captured them. In one case, a young bat was caught in the daytime and the man hung it just inside a window in his house. After dark, the mother flew in and nursed her baby and then flew off with it clinging to her fur. In another case, a baby bat was caught and carried through city streets, and the mother bat flew after the man who had it and landed on his shoulder. When he opened his hand, the mother took her baby and began to nurse it.

7 SOME BAT ODDITIES

The two big bat groups—the Microchiroptera and the Megachiroptera—divide pretty much according to the food they eat. The first are mostly insect-eaters and the second confine themselves to eating fruit and nectar. But there are several species of bats that are quite different from these. They are meat-eaters.

One of these is the fishing bat. Who would think that a bat, a creature of the air, would learn to catch fish! But after all, many birds eat fish, so why not bats? Bats do drink water and they do this by flying low over a pond or stream and lapping it up as their snouts touch the water. They

also catch insects that may be flying near the water or even swimming on the surface. So it is not surprising that bats, coming to drink and catch insects, should discover fish as a good source of food.

One bat that eats fish is *Noctilio leporinus*, which ranges from Cuba to northern Argentina. It has a close relative, *Noctilio albiventer*, which rarely eats fish but confines itself mostly to insects. Like all fish-eating bats, *N. leporinus* has unusually long and strong hind feet fitted with sharp claws. These are used to grab the fish out of the water, after which it is transferred to the bat's mouth. The insect-eating cousin has large hind feet and claws, but they are smaller than those of the true fish-eating bat. Another tropical American fishing bat is *Pizonyx* (now listed as a *Myotis* bat). This bat lives in Mexico in caves near the Gulf of Mexico. The roosting places smell strongly of fish. The bats are very shy and do their fishing at night. They seldom venture out in daylight, perhaps because of the

A Mexican fishing bat (Pizonyx vivesi) *eating a small mullet. Note this bat's huge flattened claws which it uses to snag fish from the water.* © Merlin D. Tuttle, Bat Conservation International, Milwaukee Public Museum

many predatory gulls that could easily catch a bat.

In the Old World there are other bat fishermen related to our little brown bat. They have the longer legs and big claws of all fishing bats, but not much else is known about them.

THE FROG-EATING BAT

The frog-eating bat of the American tropics is very different. Dr. Merlin D. Tuttle studied these bats on Barro Colorado Island in Panama. There, every pond has its population of frogs. All night, the males chirp and sing, trying to attract a female. But as soon as a bat approaches, all sounds cease. Dr. Tuttle wanted to learn how the bats find the frogs and also how they can distinguish between an edible frog and a poisonous frog or toad. To do this, he used a variety of techniques. He made recordings of the songs of the different species of frogs and played them outdoors at night. Bats came to the recordings of the edible frogs, sometimes sitting right on top of the playing recorder and even trying to pry open the box. But they avoided the calls of the poisonous frogs.

44

A frog-eating bat (Trachops cirrhosus) *about to catch a frog. This bat can distinguish between poisonous and edible frogs, and also locate them, by the frog calls.* © Merlin D. Tuttle, Bat Conservation International, Milwaukee Public Museum

Dr. Tuttle also found that a bat that makes a mistake and attacks a poisonous toad has a built-in warning system of its own. Around its mouth are small, bumpy protrusions, looking like skin teeth. These seem to warn the bat when

45

it has made a mistake and it backs off and leaves the poisonous toad.

To get his amazing photographs of bats and frogs, Dr. Tuttle set up a large net-covered cage in which he released captive bats. The bats quickly became tame and would fly to his hand to be fed. They showed a high degree of intelligence, and Dr. Tuttle could place a frog on a particular spot, point to it—and the bat would come and catch it when he signaled. One bat was especially good, stepping onto the scientist's hand without fear, flying to him when called, and seeming to know when he would be rewarded for good work.

Bird- and Mouse-eating Bats

Several kinds of bats eat a variety of small animals, including rodents, birds, lizards, and frogs. Such bats are carnivorous, like cats and foxes. Sometimes they even eat smaller bats. They may catch them in the air or pluck them off the walls of a cave where several species of bats may be roosting.

One of these bats is known as the false vampire. It lives in Southeast Asia and in such places as India and Australia.

46

The false vampire is among the largest of the microbats. It has a wingspread of almost two feet. It has very large, erect ears, a long, erect nose-leaf, and practically no tail. It is usually pale in color. A similar bat, found in Australia, is known as the ghost bat because of its very pale color. It lives in the northern, tropical part of the country. It is almost pure white, only the back being a very pale gray. Scientists searching through caves for these bats find the floor strewn with discarded bits of many small animals, the leftovers from the ghost bat's meal.

In Central and South America, there are three kinds of meat-eating bats: the giant spear-nosed bat, the Peters' false vampire bat, and the spear-nosed bat. The giant spear-nosed bat and the Peters' false vampire bat feed mostly on small birds and mammals. The spear-nosed bat, while usually eating insects and nectar, will eat other meat when available. The giant spear-nosed bat is the largest bat in the New World, with a wingspread of thirty inches.

Vampires

People like to scare themselves. That is why we have so many fairy tales about dragons and ogres and other monsters. One ancient monster was the vampire, a creature that sucked the blood of sleeping people. Of course, there never was such a creature, but when a blood-sucking bat was discovered in tropical America, it was promptly named the vampire. The scientific name for the vampire bat is *Desmodus*. It is a small brown bat, peculiarly adapted to its way of feeding. *Desmodus* is found only in the American tropics and nowhere else on earth. There are three closely related kinds, but *Desmodus* is the most numerous. It is a furry bat with pointed ears and a strange face. Its wingspread is about fifteen inches. It has long thumbs with two soft pads at the wrists, and it lacks a tail. The lower lip is deeply grooved and the teeth are peculiarly adapted to its way of life. The two front teeth (incisors) are long, curved, and very sharp. The canines—the pointed, doglike teeth—are also long. But the back teeth, the molars, which other animals use to grind their food, are very small, practically useless.

Desmodus lives in many places, including hollow trees and dark caves, often with other bat species. Surprisingly, it does not prey on them. Instead, it flies out at night to feed off almost any warm-blooded animal it can find. Cattle, horses, dogs, and even birds are all fair game for the vampire. Humans are just another kind of warm-blooded animal and *Desmodus* will sometimes drink human blood if people sleep out in the open.

The bat can hover in the air and alight silently on its victim. Often it lands on the ground nearby and then walks up to the animal on its long hind legs and the soft pads on its wrists. It is extremely quiet in its movement and even when it hops onto its victim and slices the skin with its razor-sharp front teeth, the other animal usually does not feel pain and awaken. The bat does not suck blood, as the legend suggests. Instead, it laps the blood as it flows from the wound. The bat's long tongue and grooved lip make a kind of drinking straw through which the blood passes into the bat's mouth.

The danger of the vampire bat is not so much its blood drinking as the diseases it may carry. True, chickens and other birds may lose so much blood from a few attacks that they die. But most large animals are not harmed by one bloodletting. Vampire bats can infect people and animals with rabies, a serious disease. There is now a life-saving inoculation against rabies, but it has to be given fairly soon after the animal or person is bitten. For ranchers, the job of inoculating tens of thousands of free-roaming cattle is almost impossible and in a rabies epidemic, whole herds may be wiped out.

Desmodus does not come into the United States. But any mammal, even cats and dogs, can become rabid. Very few of our bats do get rabies, and unlike most other animals, even these rarely become aggressive. They simply fall to the ground and die. For this reason, one should never pick up any bat, as sick ones are the ones most likely to be found. It is also a good idea to have dogs and cats inoculated against rabies. In that way, we are also protected.

BATS AND FLOWERS

Both the megabats and the microbats include species that have learned to drink nectar from flowers. Like birds and insects, they go to the flowers for the sweet liquid offered. In doing so, they pollinate the plants. Fruit-eating bats also

A dwarf epauletted bat (Micropteropus pusillus) *eating a ripe fig. Through their seed dispersal and pollination activities, bats such as this play a critical role in the survival of rain forests worldwide.* © Merlin D. Tuttle, Bat Conservation International, Milwaukee Public Museum

help the plants in this way. Probably, some fruit-eating bats discovered the sweet taste of nectar while looking for fruit among the trees. On the other hand, some scientists think that insect-eating bats pursued insects into the flowers and in doing so discovered the delights of nectar for themselves. All such bats live in tropical or subtropical areas where fruit and flowers are available throughout the year.

There are three species of nectar-feeding bats that come into our southwestern states from Mexico in the spring. They are rarely seen and turn up when least expected. They come when desert plants like agave, saguaro, and yucca have finished blooming in Mexico and are just beginning to blossom here. Like all nectar-feeding bats, they have long, thin noses and very long tongues, often with a little brush of hairs at the end.

Scientists wondered how a bat could survive on a diet of sugar and water. Research proved that only about 75 percent of their diet is nectar. Like the bees, these bats get pollen from the flowers, and pollen is so nutritious that even the small amount that the bats eat gives them the protein that all mammals need. Indeed, it has been found that the pollen of bat flowers is twice as nutritious as that of ordinary flowers.

Bat flowers open only at night when the bats are flying, and they often are white or very light colored so as to show up in the moonlight. They emit a musky smell that is attractive to bats. When the bat sticks its head into a flower, it becomes covered with sticky pollen. When it flies to the next plant and repeats the action, it leaves pollen, thus pollinating the plant. Later when cleaning itself, it swallows a good portion of the food.

Fruit-eating and nectar-feeding bats are very important to agriculture and forestry. Their work in dispersing seeds and pollinating plants is hardly appreciated by people. Getting rid of bats would be like getting rid of bees. And while bees can inflict a painful sting, bats are among the gentlest of mammals and only bite in self-defense if caught. Without them, we might not have had some very important fruits and other plant products from the tropics.

Figs, dates, avocadoes, bananas, breadfruit, and mangoes are some of these. Cashew nuts and cloves also would be missing. No more chicle latex for chewing gum. No more manila and sissal fibers for rope, no balsa wood and

other timbers. Kapok for life preservers and livestock feed would disappear. In Southeast Asia, the durian tree is prized for its delicious fruit. The crop sells for more than $100 million each year—and it is still entirely dependent on bats for survival.

Some farmers in the tropics blame the bats for eating their fruit, but in fact, the bats are usually innocent. They normally eat only fruit that is too ripe to be sold by the farmer. Fruit for the market is picked green, before it becomes attractive to bats. Most bats are really the farmers' helpers.

FINDING A HOME

While most bats seek shelter in caves or trees, a few very little bats have found unusual places to hide. One bat of the East Indies and Asia lives inside the hollow joint of a bamboo stem. It can squeeze through the tiny cracks

A cave-dwelling, nectar-eating bat (Eonycteris spelaea) *pollinating a banana flower. Flowers of the durian fruit, a cash crop valued at $112 million annually in Southeast Asia, are pollinated almost entirely by this species of bat.* © Merlin D. Tuttle, Bat Conservation International, Milwaukee Public Museum

because its head is unusually flattened. It has little suction pads on its feet and wrists that help it to cling to the smooth interior of the bamboo.

Other small bats in Africa have a habit of roosting in the nests of weaverbirds and sunbirds. These birds build basketlike nests, large and round and covered, that hang from the branches of trees. One investigator found such a deserted nest half filled with the nest of a mud wasp. But further investigation found a mother bat and two tiny babies, hiding in the upper half of the nest.

Still more surprising than this habit of taking over a bird's nest is the work of some little bats that have learned to make their own shelter. Popularly known as tent-making bats, they live in many parts of Central and South America. When in need of a resting place, they fly to a palm tree and cling to a large frond. There they bite a row of little holes across the leaf in such a way that the end portion hangs down at an angle from the main part. This makes a kind of tent in which the bats hide during the day. These are small bats and often a group of females with their young will be found resting in one leaf. Males usually roost alone in another palm-leaf tent.

Lesser short-nosed fruit bats (Cynopterus brachyotis) *roosting on a palm frond. Bats of this genus are common and widespread in Southeast Asia.*

8 THE FUTURE OF BATS

All over the world, bats are being massacred, sometimes from fear, sometimes for gain, sometimes by mistake. You might think that with the original large bat populations this would make little difference, but everywhere bat populations are declining. Caves where millions once gathered are now empty. And bats do not restore their numbers quickly, as do mice and rabbits. In most cases, bats have only one baby a year. Many species are endangered and near extinction and some are already extinct.

Like most creatures in our changing world, bats suffer from loss of habitat. But they also suffer from the senseless persecution of people who misunderstand and fear them.

Tourists and cave explorers often disturb hibernating bats, which fly away and die without their winter protection.

In Carlsbad Caverns, the bat population dropped so drastically that a large-scale study was made in 1956 by the U.S. Public Health Service. Because bats were known to contract rabies and that dread disease was turning up in our country, bats were thought to be responsible. While the study did not answer all the questions about the drop in the bat population, it did prove that rabies is rare among the creatures.

A big threat to bats is the constant spraying of poisons. DDT and other deadly insecticides are widely used against agricultural pests—and our bats are mostly insect-eaters. Just as pesticides threaten to wipe out our songbirds, they can do the same to bats. Some poisons, like DDT, are now banned in the United States, but they are still used in foreign countries, including Mexico, where they threaten bat survival. Others that are still legal here continue to kill our bats.

Another danger to cave-dwelling bats is flooding. A dam may be built some distance from a bat cave, but the rising water behind the dam can flood the cave and drown all the bats sheltering there.

Because of human activities, bats are often evicted from places where they have roosted for centuries. An abandoned mine in New Jersey was used for many years as a wintering shelter for bats. The mine was sold in 1972 and the new owners closed the entrances. The bats that arrived that fall to hibernate could not get inside. Instead, they invaded the attics of nearby homes, causing panic among the householders, who called for exterminators. Fortunately, the bats eventually found a way into the mine through some unsealed shafts.

Our country is not the only place where thoughtless destruction of bats goes on. In Thailand, bats are highly valued for food. The Khao Chong Pran Cave there has long been the source of guano mining. The bat guano from the cave supports a monastery and its school of some 460 students. The guano is sold for fertilizer, bringing in $52,860 a year. This activity also supplies jobs for the people in town. However, poachers have been trapping the bats and selling them to restaurants for 15¢ a bat. The restaurants then charge 30¢ for a bat dinner. The production of bat guano has dropped by 50 percent in five years, but the poaching still goes on and the monks seem unable to stop it. The bats are fruit bats and easily caught in nets. Other caves in Thailand that once housed thousands of bats are now empty.

Another bat, found only in Thailand, is the world's smallest mammal. The Kitti's hog-nosed bat weighs less than a penny and is about the size of a bumblebee. This unique little bat is now almost extinct, killed off to sell for tourist souvenirs.

Going farther around the world, in places like Africa, bats are threatened because tourists take their foolish fears and prejudices with them abroad. When visiting these countries, they sometimes panic when they see hundreds of fruit bats hanging in the trees outside their hotel windows. They complain to the hotel manager and the managers complain to the government, and several governments are considering bat extermination programs.

Any country that poisons its bats may be in for a lot of trouble. As we have seen, tropical bats are vital to the pro-

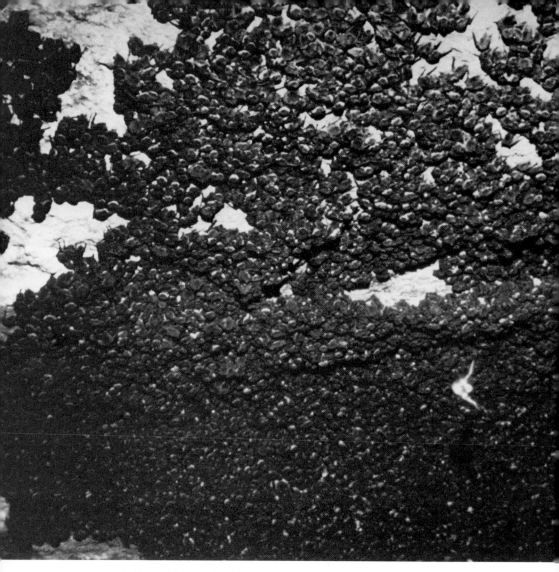

A distant cluster of endangered gray bats. Approximately 95 percent of the entire known species population of gray bats hibernate in just nine caves each winter. In these few caves dense concentrations are extremely vulnerable to human disturbance. © Merlin D. Tuttle, Bat Conservation International, Milwaukee Public Museum

duction of a host of important crops, some with annual yields of more than $100 million. And insect-eating bats are the only important predators of night-flying insects. Without bats, we would lose many important plants and trees, and we would have a far bigger plague of harmful and destructive insects to fight against. But chemical companies in this country, anxious to make more money, continue to play upon ancient fears and superstitions, both at home and abroad and urge the wholesale destruction of bats.

Should some or all bats become extinct, it would be a great loss to the world. Most bats are harmless, gentle, and very useful creatures. They are becoming helpful to medical research, especially in efforts to develop sonar for blind people. In truth, they are the wonders of the animal world, for while other mammals have learned to live on land and in the sea, only the bats are at home in the air.

INDEX